MONSTROUS MYTHS

Terrible Tales of
ANCIENT GREECE

Clare Hibbert

Gareth Stevens
Publishing

Please visit our website, www.garethstevens.com. For a free color catalog of all
our high-quality books, call toll free 1-800-542-2595 or fax 1-877-542-2596.

Library of Congress Cataloging-in-Publication Data

Hibbert, Clare.
Terrible tales of ancient Greece / by Clare Hibbert.
 p. cm. — (Monstrous myth)
Includes index.
ISBN 978-1-4824-0184-4 (pbk.)
ISBN 978-1-4824-0183-7 (6-pack)
ISBN 978-1-4824-0181-3 (library binding)
1. Mythology, Greek — Juvenile literature. I. Hibbert, Clare, 1970- II. Title.
BL783.H53 2014
292.13—dc23

First Edition

Published in 2014 by
Gareth Stevens Publishing
111 East 14th Street, Suite 349
New York, NY 10003

Copyright © 2014 Arcturus Publishing

Illustrations: Janos Jantner (Beehive Illustration)
Editor: Joe Harris
Designer: Emma Randall
Cover designer: Emma Randall

Printed in the United States of America

CPSIA compliance information: Batch #CW14GS: For further information contact Gareth Stevens, New York, New York at 1-800-542-2595.

CONTENTS

GREEK STORIES AND LEGENDS

If you could step back in time more than 2,000 years to ancient Greece, you would find yourself in a world of quarrelling gods and terrifying monsters. Or at least, that's the sort of supernatural stuff the Greeks believed in! Greece wasn't one country with one ruler, but was made up of loads of independent city-states. Each city had its own culture and laws. However, they all shared pretty much the same language (Greek, of course!) and the same stories.

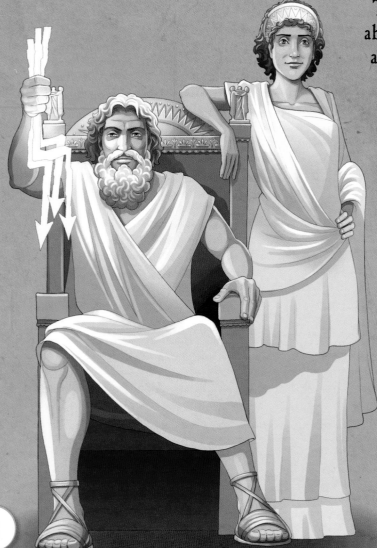

The Greeks believed in about a dozen major gods and goddesses, known as the Olympians because they lived on Mount Olympus. The Olympians could be just as moody as ordinary humans. In stories, they were constantly squabbling, putting on disguises and stirring up trouble! People made offerings to the gods to stay on their good side.

Zeus, the sky god, ruled over all the other gods. His wife Hera was the goddess of marriage.

Believe it or not!

The Greeks believed that, before the Olympians, Earth was ruled by a race of divine giants called the Titans. One of these, Cronus, was Zeus' dad. As well as the main gods, there were countless "lesser" deities, from beautiful nymphs to goaty satyrs, as well as various mixed-up creatures (centaurs were half-horse, half-man). Greek stories also featured some terrifying monsters!

Many Greek legends looked back to the "Heroic Age." There were tales of superhuman heroes, such as Heracles, Theseus, and Jason, and half-true histories of real events such as the Trojan War. The gods played a starring role in all these myths.

The god Hermes carried messages from Mount Olympus to mere mortals down below.

HERACLES THE HERO

Meet Heracles, the original superman! Even as a baby, he was tough enough to squeeze the life out of two snakes with his bare little hands. His godlike strength came from his father's side of the family: his dad was the one and only king of the gods, Zeus.

Heracles' stepmom hated him. She put those snakes in his cradle on purpose! Not your typical baby shower gift, huh?

When Heracles had grown up and had a family of his own, Hera—his stepmom—struck again. She placed poor Heracles under a spell that made him go mad and kill his beautiful wife and their six sons. Oh no! When the spell wore off, he was horrified.

Heracles visited a famous priestess, the Oracle at Delphi, to ask what his punishment for the murders should be. His sentence? To spend 12 years as the servant of his rival, King Eurystheus. As if that wasn't enough, he'd also have to complete 12 fiendishly difficult tasks. Eurystheus couldn't believe his luck. This was his chance to humiliate Heracles!

Eurystheus sent Heracles to kill a magical lion that was terrorizing the people of Nemea. No weapons could hurt this bloody beast. However, after cornering the lion in its cave, Heracles slipped one great, muscled arm around its neck. Then, with sheer brute force, he choked the creature to death. One task down, 11 to go!

After slaying the Nemean lion, Heracles wore its skin. He looked ferociously fashionable!

Heracles' next challenge was to kill the Hydra. This hideous monster had nine heads that grew back each time they were chopped off. Luckily, Heracles' nephew Iolaus lent a hand. He scorched the Hydra's necks with a flaming torch, so the heads couldn't regrow.

Tasks three and four tested the hero's hunting skills. Heracles captured the shy deer of Ceryneia and the bad-tempered boar of Mount Erymanthus.

Eurystheus realized that Heracles was doing a great job of killing monsters. So for his fifth task, he decided to embarrass him instead. He made him clean out the stinky stables of a herd of enchanted cows. But Heracles wasn't the type to get down on his knees and scrub. He changed the path of two rivers to do the job for him! After that, it was back to the monsters...

The horrible Hydra lived in a swamp.

Heracles' To-Do List

TASK 6: Scare off a flock of bloodthirsty birds. <u>*DONE!*</u>

TASK 7: Capture a magical white bull. <u>*DONE!*</u>

TASK 8: Capture some man-eating wild horses. <u>*DONE!*</u>

TASK 9: Battle the Amazons (a tribe of warrior women) and take their queen's belt. <u>*DONE!*</u>

By this point, Heracles had spent a very long time in King Eurystheus' service. For his tenth task, he had to steal a monster's cattle. This task alone took him a whole year!

His 11th task was to fetch Zeus' golden apples, which were guarded by a 100-headed dragon. Heracles tricked a Titan called Atlas into collecting them for him. Heracles' final task was kidnapping Cerberus—a three-headed, monstrous dog. He took the hideous hound to Eurystheus' palace. Heracles' rival was so scared, he didn't dare give him any more tasks!

Believe it or not!

The Romans loved the story of Heracles so much that they stole it. In their version, the hero was called Hercules.

PERSEUS AND THE SNAKE-HAIRED HORROR

Like Heracles, Perseus was a demi-god. His dad was Zeus and his mom was a princess called Danae. Like most famous heroes, Perseus was brave, strong, and incredibly good-looking. He was also absolutely devoted to his mom.

Perseus' adventure began when a king, Polydectes, took a fancy to Danae. Polydectes figured his best chance of winning Danae's hand would be to get her son off the scene. He held a feast and asked each guest to bring him some horses. Perseus didn't have any horses but boasted that he'd bring the king anything else he wanted. Polydectes was delighted. It was going to be simpler to get rid of Perseus than he'd thought. "Bring me the head of a Gorgon!" he laughed.

With snakes for hair, vicious fangs and curved claws, Gorgons were not a pretty sight.

10

A Gorgon's head? I doubt you could pick up one of those at the local store!

The Gorgons were three sisters who had snakes for hair. Worse still, they turned anyone who looked at them to stone. Two were immortal so there was no point even trying to decapitate either of them. Perseus would have to go after the mortal one, Medusa.

First Perseus tracked down a trio of old hags called the Graiae, who were sisters of the Gorgons. They shared just one eye and a tooth between them, and they had to take it in turns to use them! So Perseus stole the eye and tooth. He said he would only give them back if they gave him tips on killing Medusa. The grumbling Graiae directed Perseus to the kit he'd need: winged sandals so he could fly, an invisibility helmet, and a strong bag for carrying the Gorgon's head home.

Armed with a shiny shield—given to him by the goddess Athena, no less!—Perseus approached the Gorgons' cave. The path was lined with victims who'd been spookily turned to stone. Perseus was not going to look directly at the Gorgons, though. He would use his shield as a mirror and look only at their reflections.

Perseus crept into the cave, tiptoed right up to Medusa, and lopped off her head before she had time to cry out. Gripping her long, grisly "locks" (actually nasty, writhing snakes), he plopped the head into the bag. Yuck!

Perseus' helmet was magic. It made him invisible to the Gorgons!

At that moment, Medusa's hideous sisters woke and flew at Perseus in a rage. Perseus could fly, thanks to his sandals, but so could the Gorgons—and he wasn't sure he could outfly them. Luckily he remembered his helmet. He put it on and—poof!—he vanished. The ghastly Gorgons had to give up their chase.

Perseus had one more adventure on his journey back home. Flying over the sea, he came across a beautiful princess, Andromeda, chained to a rock. She was there as a sacrifice for Cetus, a sea monster. The monster was too big for Perseus to fight, but the hero had a cunning plan. He whipped Medusa's head out of the sack, and its gaze turned Cetus to stone. Then Perseus unchained the princess and asked her to marry him. Andromeda's answer? "Yes!," of course!

Believe it or not!

The Greeks named two constellations (patterns of stars) after Perseus and Andromeda. They lie side by side in the night sky. Andromeda's stars make the figure of the princess with arms outstretched. Perseus holds up his sword and Medusa's head.

HUNT FOR THE GOLDEN FLEECE

The hero Jason had an unusual upbringing. He should have had a charmed life as the prince of Iolcos. But his power-crazed uncle, Pelias, seized the throne when he was a boy and imprisoned his dad. Jason had to be brought up in secret far away so that his uncle couldn't kill him.

When he was grown up, Jason returned to Iolcos. The first thing he did on arriving was help an old woman cross a river. The woman was really the goddess Hera in disguise! While Jason was helping her, he lost a sandal. He didn't know that an oracle had told his uncle to beware of a man wearing one sandal...

Jason's ship, the Argo, was powered by sails and oars. Its name meant "swift."

Pelias realized who Jason was but had no intention of giving up his kingship. He sneakily promised the throne to Jason if he brought him a famous treasure: the priceless Golden Fleece.

The Golden Fleece belonged to King Aeëtes, who ruled the faraway state of Colchis. Jason had a boat built, the *Argo*, and assembled a crew of about 50 to man it. They were known as the Argonauts, and included the heroes Heracles, Perseus, and Theseus.

There was never a dull moment on the journey to Colchis. First, the Argonauts spent a lovely time on Lemnos, an island inhabited only by women. Next they stayed with Cyzicua, the kind king of the Dolionians. While there, the Argonauts had to fight off a raid by six-armed giants. But when the Argonauts set off once more for Colchis, a storm blew them back, and they ended up accidentally doing battle with the Dolionians. There's gratitude for you!

Pelias was sure that he had seen the last of Jason. He thought the quest would be impossible...

Next Jason ran into another king—old, blind Phineus of Thrace. Jason and his crew killed the monstrous Harpies that were stealing Phineus' food. In return, the king told Jason how to pass through the next hazard along his journey: vice-like cliffs that had a habit of crushing any ship that sailed through them.

Finally Jason and the Argonauts arrived at Colchis. King Aeëtes didn't want to hand over the Golden Fleece, but said he would give it to Jason if he performed a special task. Fortunately, Jason had some help on the inside—from Aeëtes' lovestruck daughter!

The Golden Fleece was guarded by a sleepless dragon.

My Secret Diary by Princess Medea

Today Dad had the dreamiest visitor. His name's Jason, and he's after the Golden Fleece. Dad says that he can have it if he ploughs a field with his royal bulls and sows it with dragons' teeth. Jason doesn't realize that the bulls breathe fire or that warriors will spring from the dragons' teeth. Luckily I've slipped him a magical ointment to protect against the bulls' breath. I've told him how to trick the warriors into fighting each other, too!

Aeëtes was very angry when Jason completed the challenge. So—surprise, surprise!—he refused to hand over the fleece. The Golden Fleece was guarded by a dragon that never slept, but Medea had the answer. She concocted a sleeping potion for the dragon, so Jason could snatch the fleece and she could sail away with him.

Back on Iolcos, Pelias had no intention of giving up the throne, but he hadn't reckoned on Jason's new girlfriend! Rebellious Medea managed to persuade Pelias' daughters to chop him up—so he met a very grisly end indeed.

Believe it or not!

According to legend, the Golden Fleece had belonged to a winged ram, which was one of the sea god Poseidon's children. This ram later became the constellation Aries.

LOCKING HORNS WITH THE MINOTAUR

Holy cow! You wouldn't want to mess with this mythical monster. Normal bulls might happily munch on grass, but the bull-headed Minotaur had an insatiable appetite for human flesh. It lived on the island of Crete in a maze called the Labyrinth.

The best-known myth about the Minotaur describes what it ate and how its lunch learned to fight back! The story begins when the son of King Minos, the ruler of Crete, was killed in a war with Athens.

The Minotaur of Crete was a fearsome, flesh-eating monster.

No wonder the Minotaur was so royally mixed up! His mom was a queen... and his dad was a bull.

Crete eventually won the war, and King Minos devised a truly twisted way to take revenge for the death of his son. Every year, he decreed, the Athenians would have to send seven boys and seven girls to Crete. Minos would lock them inside the Labyrinth, where they would wander until they eventually met the Minotaur. Then the bull-headed brute would tuck into an all-you-can-eat people picnic.

This terrible tradition carried on for many years, until someone eventually decided that enough was enough. Who was that someone? Why, no other than the king of Athens' own son, Theseus. Prince Theseus had an idea. He would join the young people being sent to Crete, and—using nothing but his own smarts—slay the horrible creature.

Theseus didn't have much of a plan, but he didn't tell his dad that! He was hoping for help from the gods or a miracle. The miracle turned out to be Minos' daughter, Ariadne. Theseus met her at a party her dad threw. Minos wasn't a total meanie—if the youngsters were destined to become Minotaur munchies, they might as well enjoy their last night.

Ariadne was bored stiff on Crete and saw that Theseus was her ticket off the island. She promised to help him kill the Minotaur if he'd take her away. Deal! Ariadne gave Theseus two gifts to hide just inside the Labyrinth—a ball of string and a sword.

Theseus killed the Minotaur with the sword that Ariadne had given him.

Minos' guards led the seven boys and seven girls to the Labyrinth. Theseus left the others by the door, tying one end of his string there. Then he set off. He found the Minotaur sleeping at the center of the maze. They fought hard, but Theseus was the winner. Having killed the beast with Ariadne's sword, he used the string to retrace his steps.

On the journey home, Theseus stopped at the island of Naxos. There, the goddess Athena advised him to leave Ariadne behind. Theseus didn't dare to argue with a goddess, but in his rush to get going, he forgot to change his black sail for a white one. A white one would show his dad he'd survived. His dad was so grief-stricken when he saw the black-sailed ship approaching that he threw himself into the sea. Not the perfect homecoming...but it did mean that Theseus became king of Athens!

Believe it or not!

What happened to the beautiful Ariadne? She married Dionysus, the god of wine, and became an immortal goddess.

HOW A HORSE ENDED A WAR

How does an epic ten-year war begin? Well, the Trojan War began with a beauty contest. Not just any beauty contest, a divine one, between the goddesses Aphrodite, Athena, and Hera. They asked Paris, the prince of Troy, to judge which of them was the most beautiful and give the winner a golden apple. Paris chose Aphrodite, the goddess of love, and she rewarded him by saying he could marry the most beautiful woman in the world.

As a prince, Paris was used to getting his own way. He didn't expect to start a war...

Sounds straightforward enough? Well, not really. The most beautiful woman in the world was Helen, and she was already married to Menelaus, the king of Sparta. But Paris wasn't going to let a little detail like that get in the way! Aphrodite made sure Helen fell in love with Paris, and they sailed away to Troy.

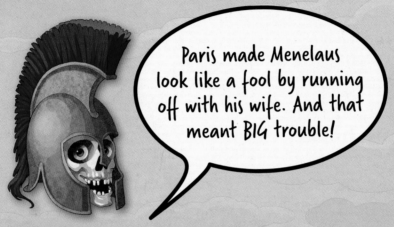

Paris made Menelaus look like a fool by running off with his wife. And that meant BIG trouble!

Menelaus' brother Agamemnon gathered together all the Greek leaders and made them join him in a war on Paris' home city of Troy. For Agamemnon, the insult was personal. Helen was his sister-in-law twice over—as his brother's wife and also his own wife's sister!

The Greek forces included hundreds of ships and some of the bravest warriors of the day: Achilles, Ajax, Diomedes, and Odysseus. However, the Trojans had their own heroes, including Paris' brother Hector and another prince of Troy, Aeneas. They also had a huge great wall protecting their city.

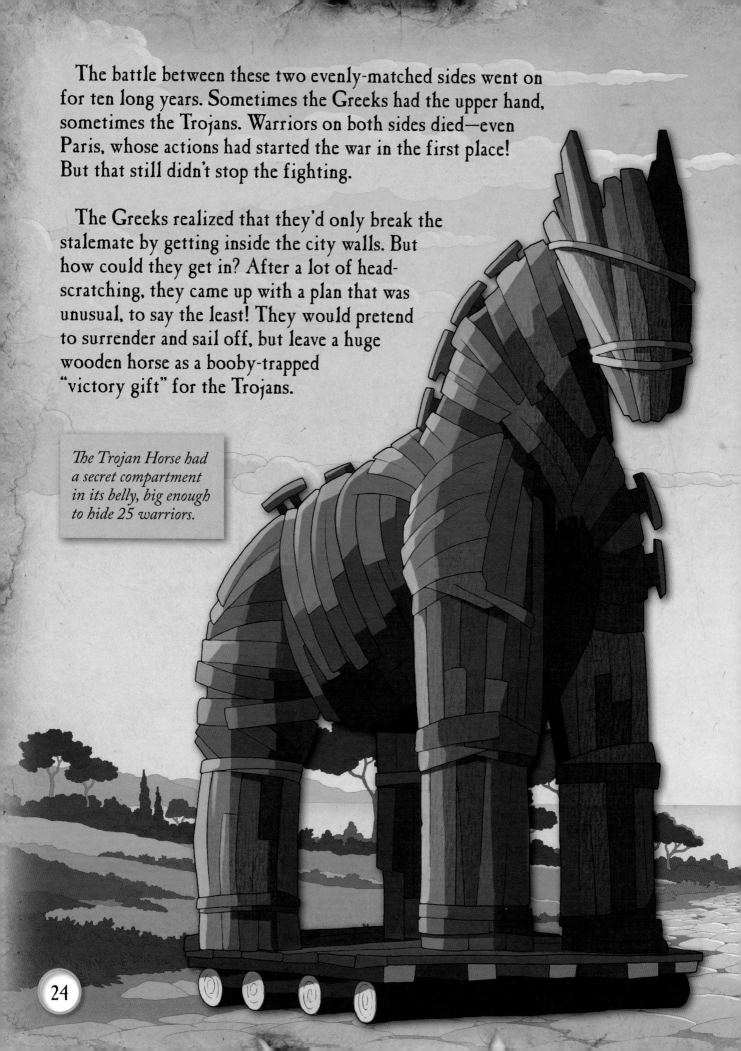

The battle between these two evenly-matched sides went on for ten long years. Sometimes the Greeks had the upper hand, sometimes the Trojans. Warriors on both sides died—even Paris, whose actions had started the war in the first place! But that still didn't stop the fighting.

The Greeks realized that they'd only break the stalemate by getting inside the city walls. But how could they get in? After a lot of head-scratching, they came up with a plan that was unusual, to say the least! They would pretend to surrender and sail off, but leave a huge wooden horse as a booby-trapped "victory gift" for the Trojans.

The Trojan Horse had a secret compartment in its belly, big enough to hide 25 warriors.

A Letter Home from the Front

Penelope, my dear wife and queen,
Yours truly has come up with a plan for victory. I've made the men build a big wooden horse for some of us to hide in while everyone else sails off out of sight. Hopefully those Trojan simpletons will think we've given up and take in the horse. If all goes to plan I should be back with you very soon.
All my love, Odysseus xxx

The Trojans fell for the trick. They wheeled the horse into the city and began celebrating victory. Once everyone was asleep, Odysseus and his men crept out of the horse's belly and opened the gate to their fellow Greeks. By morning, Troy had fallen. Even Priam, Troy's king, was dead.

The Greeks won the war—but at a terrible cost. Over the course of the war, most had managed to annoy the gods at one time or another and they paid the price. Some died after storms sank their ships; others wandered lost for years. Only Agamemnon made it home swiftly, but his wife had got fed up waiting for him. On his first night back, she had him murdered—not exactly the welcome he'd been expecting!

Believe it or not!

The likely site of the real Troy is Hisarlik, a large mound in northwestern Anatolia, Turkey. Archaeologists have found the ruins of an ancient citadel there.

THE LONGEST JOURNEY HOME EVER!

Although Odysseus was one of the great heroes of the Trojan War, he'd never wanted to take part in the fighting. He even pretended to be crazy because he was desperate not to leave his wife and baby son.

On the journey home from Troy, disaster struck almost at once when a massive storm blew Odysseus' ships off course. They washed up on the island home of the Lotus-Eaters, strange folk who fed on flowers that made them super-sleepy. When Odysseus' men tasted the flowers, they lost all interest in everything. Poor Odysseus had to carry them to the ships.

Odysseus' journey home was far from a pleasure cruise. He had to face monsters like this giant one-eyed Cyclops.

Next, the men reached an island of one-eyed giants called Cyclopes. A Cyclops called Polyphemus trapped Odysseus and a dozen of his best men in a cave. Polyphemus really liked Greek food—Greek sailors, that is!

Six men were eaten before Odysseus came up with an escape plan. First he blinded the monster by driving a pointy stick into its eye. Then, he and his men clung to the bellies of the Cyclops' flock of sheep and goats as they were let out to graze. Free at last!

At their next island stop-off, Odysseus was given a magical sack of wind. Thanks to this breezy bag, the fleet was soon in sight of his home, Ithaca. But then some of the men opened the bag. Big mistake! They were blown right back where they'd started. Drat.

Poor Odysseus! He was desperate to get home... but he was away from his kingdom for 20 years!

The ships stopped for supplies at an island where giant cannibals lived. By the time they realized the danger, it was too late. Eleven of the ships and their crews became cannibals' canapés. Only Odysseus' ship survived.

Scylla snatched six men as Odysseus' ship sailed close by and ate them alive.

The next stop was Aeaea, home to the beautiful sorceress Circe. Her top trick was transforming people into beasts. She laid out a fabulous feast for the worn-out sailors, but their pigging out turned them into pigs. Only Odysseus escaped the spell. With the help of the goddess Athena, he changed the swine back into sailors.

After a quick trip to the edge of the world to pay their respects to the dead, the men had to pass the Sirens, enchanting creatures whose songs lured sailors to their deaths. Everyone except Odysseus blocked their ears with wax. He wanted to hear the singing, but to stay safe from mischief, he was tied to the mast for that part of the journey. The next challenge was to chart a course between Charybdis, a wicked whirlpool that could swallow a ship, and the six-headed monster Scylla. The sea monster gobbled up six of Odysseus' men.

On the island Thrinakia, Odysseus' hungry men disobeyed him and ate some of the sun god's cattle. Their punishment was yet more delay, years trapped on the nymph Calypso's island. When Odysseus finally reached home, he found his palace overrun with men competing to marry his queen. Odysseus killed the lot of them—with a little help from his grown-up son—and settled back to enjoy life with his wife at long last.

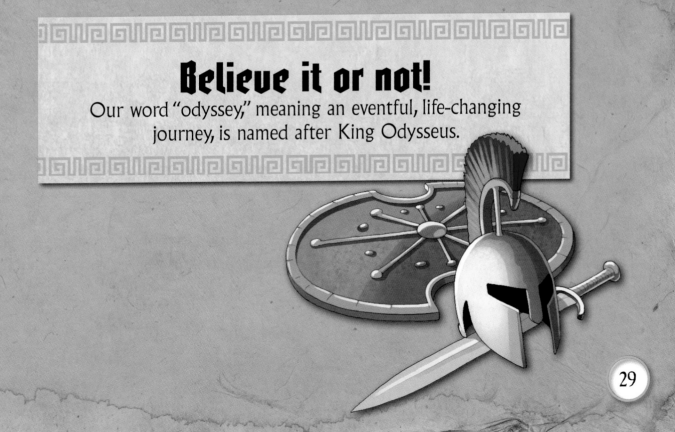

Believe it or not!

Our word "odyssey," meaning an eventful, life-changing journey, is named after King Odysseus.

GLOSSARY

city-state A city and its surrounding countryside, which together made up an independent state. Athens and Sparta were two of the most famous ancient Greek city-states.

civilization A stable human society where the people have developed a form of government and have organized religion, writing, technology, trade, and buildings.

constellation A section of sky where the stars form an imaginary pattern, such as the body of a human or animal.

decapitate To chop off someone or something's head.

deity A god or goddess.

divine Like a god, or belonging to a god.

immortal A being that will live forever. Gods are immortal; humans are mortal (they will die).

Minotaur A beast that had the head of a bull and the body of a man, and was kept in a maze on the island of Crete.

nymph A minor goddess who has power over woodlands, rivers, or other features of nature.

Olympian One of the main Greek gods and goddesses that lived on Mount Olympus.

oracle A priest or priestess who can speak on behalf of a god, or the sacred site where they live.

quarrel To argue or disagree.

satyr A wood spirit.

Siren A beautiful woman who lives in or by the sea, singing enchanting songs that tempt sailors into the water to their deaths.

sorceress A woman who can cast magic spells.

Titan A member of the race of giant creatures that ruled Earth before the Olympians.

vice-like Describes two things that can squeeze or crush objects between them.

FURTHER INFORMATION

Further Reading

Greek Myths by Ann Turnbull (Candlewick, 2011)

The Lost Hero by Rick Riordan (Puffin, 2011)

The Odyssey by Gillian Cross (Candlewick, 2012)

Theseus and the Minotaur by Hugh Lupton (Barefoot Books, 2013)

Treasury of Greek Mythology by Donna Jo Napoli (National Geographic Society, 2011)

The Usborne Book of Greek Myths by Anna Milbourne (Usborne, 2010)

Websites

www.ancientgreece.co.uk
A website produced by the British Museum that explores the world of ancient Greece through objects in the museum's collection.

www.bbc.co.uk/learningzone/clips/anthony-horowitz-the-gorgons-head/6877.html
A dramatization of the Perseus and Medusa myth, as retold by top author Anthony Horowitz.

www.mythweb.com/heroes/heroes.html
Animated biographies of six heroes of Greek mythology.

www.pantheon.org/areas/mythology/europe/greek/
The part of the comprehensive online Encyclopedia Mythica that explores Greek gods and stories.

www.storynory.com/category/educational-and-entertaining-stories/greek-myths/
A website with three pages of links to classic Greek stories, each supplied as text and with an audio clip.

INDEX